# *Mary Anning*
## Fossil Hunter

## by Annie Temple

HOUGHTON MIFFLIN          BOSTON

Here is an old tongue twister. Can you say it three times fast?

*She sells seashells by the seashore.*

Some people think this tongue twister is about a real woman who lived about two hundred years ago. Mary Anning was born in a small town in England in 1799. She really did sell seashells by the seashore. She also helped change our understanding of the history of life on Earth. Here is her story.

Mary Anning lived in Lyme Regis, a small town on the south coast of England.

## A Childhood by the Sea

When Mary was a child, she used to walk with her father by the sea near her home. They would pick up "curiosities," strange stone-like objects they found on the beach. They polished these things up and gave them interesting names, such as "crocodilian snouts," "ladies' fingers," and "snake stones." Then they sold them at Mr. Anning's carpentry shop.

What were these strange things? No one knew. When Mary was a child, most people knew nothing about fossils. They couldn't imagine that life on earth had changed over time. The word "dinosaur" didn't even exist. How could anyone know that they were actually fossils—remains of animals that lived millions of years earlier, but were now extinct?

People liked to buy the curiosities, though. Tourists bought them to remember their vacation at the beach. Scientists bought them too.

It is easy to see why ammonite fossils were called "snake stones."

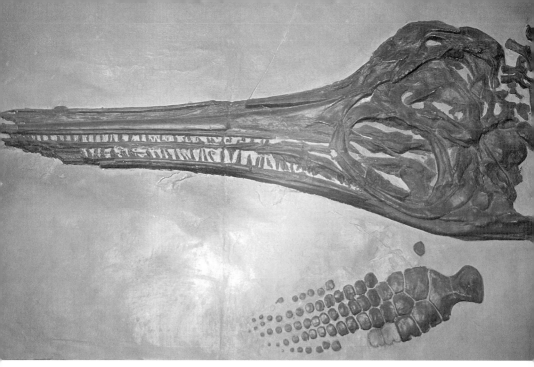

Joseph Anning found a skull that seemed to belong to a crocodile.

# An Important Discovery

Mary's father died when she was ten or eleven. Because her family didn't have much money, she continued to hunt for fossils to sell. Her older brother, Joseph, helped her. They climbed on cliffs near the ocean and hammered at the rock. When Mary was about twelve, she and her brother made a big discovery.

Joseph uncovered something that looked like the skull of a giant crocodile. It had long jaws and lots of sharp teeth.

A year later, Mary found a piece of a backbone in the same area. She dug around that fossil and found a rib. With help, she uncovered the rest of the fossil. It was the skeleton of an ancient sea-going reptile. The skeleton was almost seventeen feet long.

The Annings sold that fossil and got a lot of money for it. Mary also developed a hunger for learning. She studied the fossils she found. She drew what she observed. She examined the cliffs where she found them. And she kept hunting for more.

**A complete skeleton of an ichthyosaur, which means "fish lizard"**

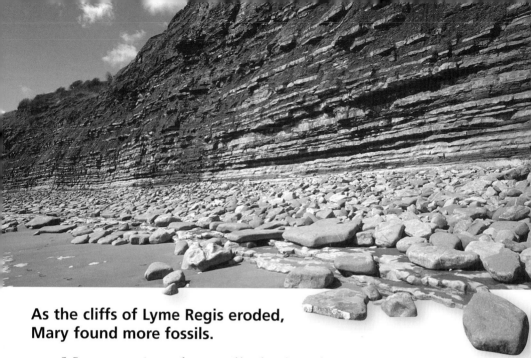

**As the cliffs of Lyme Regis eroded,
Mary found more fossils.**

Mary continued to walk the beach most days, in every season, in all kinds of weather. Sometimes she went with her brother or a friend. Sometimes she took her dog.

The wind, rain, and tides helped Mary. The cliffs near her beach were made up of many thin layers of soft rock and clay. This rock was easily worn away. As the soil washed away, fossils were exposed.

Fossil hunting could be dangerous. There were mudslides. The cliffs were steep. If she didn't pay attention, Mary could get trapped by the high tide. But the cliffs held fossils and Mary wanted to discover more of them. She wanted to learn everything she could about them.

In the early 1800s, people didn't think women could be scientists. Poor girls like Mary couldn't afford to spend much time in school. Instead, Mary learned by talking to people about the curiosities. Friends loaned her books about geology so she could find out more about rocks. She read papers and books written about fossils by paleontologists (scientists who study ancient life). She even taught herself French, because some of the books about fossils were written in that language. Mostly, though, Mary learned by observing.

**Mary learned about fossils at the beach, not in a schoolhouse.**

# A Woman Scientist

While Mary was discovering fossils, paleontologists were discovering her. They came to her small town. At first they knew her as a good fossil hunter. They trusted her to find the best fossils. They knew she would dig them out carefully and clean them well. They knew she could put the pieces of a skeleton together correctly.

Soon they discovered she also had a good understanding of animals that lived long ago. Even though she hadn't spent much time in school, she could teach the paleontologists about her discoveries. She wasn't afraid to argue with them. One person wrote that she knew more about fossils than anyone else.

**William Buckland, geologist, visited Mary to learn more about fossils.**

In 1823, Mary dug up a different kind of skeleton. It had a small head, like a turtle. Its neck seemed to belong to a big snake. It had paddles, not legs. No one had ever seen anything like it.

Some experts believed this was another ancient sea animal. Others declared it was a fake. No animal could ever look like that, they said. With such a long neck, how would it be able to hold up its head? They believed Mary had taken fossils from different animals and put them together to fool paleontologists. As the scientists argued, Mary worried. Would they ever trust her again?

The experts discussed Mary's fossil at a special meeting. Some pointed to a crack in the neck. Had Mary mixed two skeletons together? Some pointed to the tiny head. How could a creature with such a small brain survive?

But other paleontologists were sure Mary's find was from a kind of animal that was now extinct. They had bits of fossils that matched parts of the skeleton Mary had found. They could describe how this animal must have lived. In the end, people were convinced the skeleton was real.

**Mary Anning found the first complete skeleton of the plesiosaur.**

# A Hard Life

Now the experts respected Mary Anning. Still, life wasn't easy for Mary and her family. They never had much money.

Mary was good at selling the fossils. She knew how to polish them and display them well. But being a fossil hunter wasn't an easy way to earn a living. Other people in her town sold fossils, too. Sometimes she sent fossils to museums, but never got paid. Some years, money was tight and no one could afford to buy fossils.

Mary kept collecting, though. She uncovered fossils of flying reptiles with wings and teeth. She found fossils of squid-like animals. When she cut these open, she discovered pockets of dried ink inside. A friend ground up the fossil-ink and drew pictures of ancient animals with it.

Mary even found fossils of the droppings of ancient animals. By studying them, she learned the foods some ancient reptiles ate. She also began to understand how fossils were made.

**Pterodactylus fossil**

**An artist drew this picture to show what "The Age of Reptiles" might have looked like.**

Because of Mary's discoveries, people could imagine what life once was like. One scientist drew a picture of an ancient sea. It showed the crocodile-like creature eating the turtle-headed creature. Winged reptiles flew above them in the sky. He sold copies of this picture and gave the money to Mary.

Other scientists saw all that Mary had done to help them understand ancient life. They decided to give her a small amount of money every year.

She wasn't considered a real scientist in those days, though. How could she be? She was a woman. She hadn't had much schooling. And she was a worker, a fossil hunter. The people who bought fossils from her and then donated them to museums got most of the credit.

One way of being honored is to have a fossil named after you. Mary Anning had very few fossils named after her. Not a single reptile she discovered was given her name. Even a tongue twister that *might* be about her doesn't mention her by name.

**Artist's illustration of what two ichthyosaurs might have looked like more than 200 million years ago**

Still, we know now how much Mary Anning accomplished in her life. She worked hard to support her family. She learned everything she could about the fossils she uncovered and what they told her about ancient life. She taught herself to be a scientist.

The discoveries Mary made helped people think about how life on Earth has changed over time. Because of the fossils she uncovered, people could picture the plants and animals in ancient seas. Mary Anning did a lot more than sell seashells by the seashore!